www.welcometosmallhouse.com
www.mazdamiles.com

ISBN: 979 8 985 9656 1 2

First Edition

how
to use
this
journal

Society has taught us, particularly women, to focus on love outwardly. Although self-love has become a catchphrase, taking the actual time to go within and intentionally love ourselves from the inside out is an entirely different thing. This journal is designed to guide and aid you in the journey of exploring love—self-love—from a practical perspective.

Each entry will focus on one aspect of what is known as the Bible's "Love Chapter" (1 Corinthians 13). Corresponding journal prompts are provided for you to introspectively reflect on how you can begin to love yourself more profoundly.

Day One

Love is PATIENT.

The Greek word in this passage is *makrothumeó* which means long-tempered (to defer anger), refusing to retaliate with anger because of human reasoning. So, when one acts in love, which is patient, they have the capacity to have been done wrong and NOT retaliate.

If we're honest, we've consistently punished ourselves for things we did wrong or for not living up to the prescribed standards. No one is harder on us than we are on ourselves! Think about it, the random thoughts daily, "Oh, I shouldn't have done that!" and "If I would've just thought about it this way," or "Leave it to me to screw things up!" And then, after we've said all of those things, we ruminate on all of the reasons we don't deserve better in our lives. Are we showing self-love in these moments?

Yet when a friend, family member, or child does the same, we are quick to come to their rescue, console them, and tell them that they absolutely did their best. We have patience with them. We can make their mistakes make sense, but not our own. It's time for that to stop. Because on this love journey, we are required—commanded, even—to prioritize SELF.

Today, I challenge you to consider ways in which you can be more patient with yourself. I challenge you to arrest each punishing and retaliating thought before it can turn into action. I challenge you to extend yourself the long-suffering support you show so many others because you are worthy of the same. *That's love.*

Reflections

1. As you enter this journey to profound self-love, how would you describe your current self- love scenario?

Reflections

2. What did today's entry reveal to you about how you love yourself, and how did that make you feel?

_____

_____

_____

_____

_____

_____

_____

_____

_____

_____

_____

_____

_____

Reflections

3. What is one practical way to apply these concepts immediately to your life while building on what you've previously learned?

Day Two

Love is KIND.

Chrésteuomai is a Greek word meaning to do good and be useful. Think about that from a self-love perspective. Are we doing good and being useful to ourselves? Do you speak to yourself in a useful way? Do you take care of your mind, body, and spirit in a good and useful way? We say and do a lot, but the usefulness of those words and actions should be called into question. How many times have we said, "That wasn't necessary," to someone else but aren't willing to say it to ourselves? It's time to consider if we are *truly* kind to ourselves, and if so, are we *as kind* to ourselves as we are to others?

I challenge you to consider if your words about yourself are useful. Are the thoughts that live rent-free in your mind about yourself useful? I challenge you to speak, live, and move, perpetuating good and useful thoughts and actions to yourself, for yourself. *That's* love.

Reflections

1. How did you apply yesterday's concept to your life, and how did that work out?

_____
_____
_____
_____
_____
_____
_____
_____
_____
_____
_____
_____
_____
_____
_____

Reflections

2. What did today's entry reveal to you about how you love yourself, and how did that make you feel?

Reflections

3. What is one practical way to apply these concepts immediately to your life while building on what you've previously learned?

_____
_____
_____
_____
_____
_____
_____
_____
_____
_____
_____
_____
_____
_____
_____

Day Three

Love is not ENVIOUS.

Translated from the Greek word *zéloó*, envious means "eager to possess." We know that we should not be eager to possess the things of others, but let's take a closer look at our relationship with God and ourselves. We glorify being proactive, tenacious, and rigorous in pursuit of our future, but at what point does our eagerness turn AGAINST our self-love? "I should have had this by now. I should have done that by now. I should have accomplished this by now." Is *that* living in love? Today, I challenge us to take inventory of the things we have been so eager to possess that we have turned them into self-loathing moments instead of being patient and kind to ourselves in the process and journey of life.

I challenge you to take a moment to CELEBRATE what has already been possessed and commit to loving yourself through the journey of attaining everything else. *That's* love.

Reflections

1. How did you apply yesterday's concept to your life, and how did that work out?

Reflections

2. What did today's entry reveal to you about how you love yourself, and how did that make you feel?

_____

_____

_____

_____

_____

_____

_____

_____

_____

_____

_____

_____

_____

_____

Reflections

3. What is one practical way to apply these concepts immediately to your life while building on what you've previously learned?

Day Four

Love is not BOASTFUL.

The Greek word in this passage is *perpereuomai*, which means to be a braggart, needing and seeking too much attention. So, self-love cannot be about running around loudly bragging about how much we love ourselves and how great we are for doing so. We know that many get this confused and do precisely that, thinking it's proof that they truly love themselves. However, when we genuinely love ourselves, we won't need to shout it from the mountaintops because we'd be secure in that love. Usually, this need to loudly affirm our self-love is precisely the opposite—a cry for help and telling of our dissatisfaction and a deflection from our truth. Further, when we practice self-love, we are not excessive in our need for attention from others. Our love is enough!

If you find yourself in a place where you are craving more attention from others, challenge yourself with this: Am I giving MYSELF enough attention? Am I focusing on MYSELF enough so that I don't crave attention and validation from others?

I challenge you to take inventory of your love for yourself and then love yourself enough to BE ENOUGH of what you need for yourself. *That's* love.

Reflections

1. How did you apply yesterday's concept to your life, and how did that work out?

_____

_____

_____

_____

_____

_____

_____

_____

_____

_____

_____

_____

_____

_____

Reflections

2. What did today's entry reveal to you about how you love yourself, and how did that make you feel?

Reflections

3. What is one practical way to apply these concepts immediately to your life while building on what you've previously learned?

_____

_____

_____

_____

_____

_____

_____

_____

_____

_____

_____

_____

_____

_____

_____

Day Five

Love is not PUFFED UP.

This Greek word, *phusioó*, means to inflate and to blow up. By inference, this means to appear larger than it actually is. So let's rephrase with this understanding: Love is not inflated; love is not blown out of proportion. Love is what it is, and it is ENOUGH. Slightly different than being boastful and making noise (bragging) for attention, being puffed up is doing THINGS to appear larger than yourself to get the attention. While we were challenged about not shouting from the mountaintops how much we are in love with ourselves to gain attention, what about the things we do *without saying a word* that are ultimately to the same end?

So today, we address the motives for our actions. Are we working out, starting a business, seeking promotion, going on vacation, getting a massage, losing weight, or having self-care days in the name of LOOKING like we love ourselves? Or are we REALLY loving ourselves? And by really loving yourself, I mean loving where you are RIGHT NOW in your journey, not the inflated version of yourself you've chosen to put on display. So I ask you—will you love the RIGHT NOW you? You may be smaller than you want to be, but the call to action then is to GROW into who you were destined to be, not falsely inflate yourself for the sake of the world's opinion.

Today I challenge you to take inventory of your ACTIONS and ensure your motives are for you and not others. And again, love yourself enough to BE ENOUGH of what you need TO BE, to yourself. Repeat after me: I AM ENOUGH. *That's* love.

Reflections

1. How did you apply yesterday's concept to your life, and how did that work out?

Reflections

2. What did today's entry reveal to you about how you love yourself, and how did that make you feel?

_____

_____

_____

_____

_____

_____

_____

_____

_____

_____

_____

_____

_____

_____

_____

Reflections

3. What is one practical way to apply these concepts immediately to your life while building on what you've previously learned?

Day Six

Love does not act UNBECOMINGLY.

The root word from which *aschémoneó* (the Greek word translated to unbecomingly) means "without proper shape or form." So, a better way to say this is love does not call you to STEP OUTSIDE of yourself and your character. Further, SELF-love doesn't call you to step out of who you know you are and come out of character for the sake of others. So often, when faced with opposition, hurt, defeat, contention, or betrayal, we are tempted to step outside of ourselves and our character to face these moments. Sometimes we are tempted to step outside of ourselves and the essence of the fearfully and wonderfully made humans we are just because we want to fit in and find acceptance.

But what does that say about how we love ourselves? We must love ourselves enough to know that WE are enough to handle situations while remaining in OUR OWN character and form. We must also accept this truth: anyone who needs you to be ANOTHER you is not WORTHY of you.

Today, I challenge you to consider the last time you stepped outside of yourself and rewrite that script. Commit to showing up as your authentic, sufficient self! *That's* love.

Reflections

1. How did you apply yesterday's concept to your life, and how did that work out?

Reflections

2. What did today's entry reveal to you about how you love yourself, and how did that make you feel?

Reflections

3. What is one practical way to apply these
concepts immediately to your life while building
on what you've previously learned?

_____
_____
_____
_____
_____
_____
_____
_____
_____
_____
_____
_____
_____
_____
_____

Day Seven

Love does not seek it's OWN.

While it may seem counterintuitive, self-love is not SELFISH. The Greek in this passage, *zéteó heautou,* means: to seek by inquiring; to investigate to reach a binding (terminal) resolution; to search, "getting to the bottom of a matter" of himself, herself, or itself.

Loving myself doesn't mean only thinking of *myself.* I've seen time and time again, people who have fallen on the journey of self-love say, "That's it... from now on, it's ALL ABOUT ME!!!" But here's the rub: as humans, we were created to need companionship, friendship, and relationship, so cutting off the rich and fulfilling connections one has in an effort to love yourself, is actually an act of violence against yourself. Read that again! So many times, we take the "it's all about me stance" when we've been (ab)used or (mis)used, forgetting that we were created to BE used.

YES, love yourself and seek out the best for yourself. YES, to digging deep and loving yourself beyond measure, but continue to share what you've received in the process. If your brother or sister is struggling with getting to the bottom of their matters, love on them too. Self-love is NOT selfish. On this quest, be sure to keep your love well-rounded. *That's* love.

Reflections

1. How did you apply yesterday's concept to your life, and how did that work out?

_____

_____

_____

_____

_____

_____

_____

_____

_____

_____

_____

_____

_____

_____

_____

_____

_____

Reflections

2. What did today's entry reveal to you about how you love yourself, and how did that make you feel?

_____

_____

_____

_____

_____

_____

_____

_____

_____

_____

_____

_____

_____

_____

Reflections

3. What is one practical way to apply these concepts immediately to your life while building on what you've previously learned?

Day Eight

Love does not PROVOKE.

The Greek word used here, *paroxynetai*, means to cut close alongside a sharp edge, sharpen, or irritate. We know we ought not to provoke and irritate others, but how do we treat ourselves? We have embraced the theory of sharpening ourselves to get to the next level, but have we *really* considered what and *who* we sacrifice in the process?

Knife sharpening is the process of making the blade sharp by GRINDING against a hard, rough surface. We subscribe so easily to the theory that the "grind" doesn't sleep and is necessary to attain all of our dreams—it's time to level up. Are we grinding our obstacles or grinding ourselves? Who is really on the butcher's block as we *grind*?

I challenge you to take inventory of the ways that you are potentially grinding yourself in pursuit of success and redirect that energy toward the obstacles. I challenge you to take yourself off the butcher's block and offer grace instead. *That's* love.

Reflections

1. How did you apply yesterday's concept to your life, and how did that work out?

_____
_____
_____
_____
_____
_____
_____
_____
_____
_____
_____
_____
_____
_____
_____

Reflections

2. What did today's entry reveal to you about how you love yourself, and how did that make you feel?

Reflections

3. What is one practical way to apply these concepts immediately to your life while building on what you've previously learned?

Day Nine

Love does not RECKON WRONGS.

The Greek word used there is *logizomai*, from the root word logos, meaning to consider, think, and reason. This is the same word from which our English words "logic" and "logical" are derived. So, more accurately translated: love does not try to make sense of wrong, and it does not try to reason to come to a logical conclusion.

How often do we make excuses for ourselves and others and call it love? Love does not try to make sense of wrong— wrong is wrong. We must FORGIVE wrong, but making excuses for wrong is a disservice to ourselves and others. SELF-love is also FACING yourself, SEEING yourself (even when it's ugly), LOVING yourself, FORGIVING yourself, and COMMITTING to yourself to do better.

Today, I challenge you to consider some of the ways you've made excuses for yourself instead of committing to change for your own good. Love on yourself today by holding yourself accountable. *That's love.*

Reflections

1. How did you apply yesterday's concept to your life, and how did that work out?

Reflections

2. What did today's entry reveal to you about how you love yourself, and how did that make you feel?

Reflections

3. What is one practical way to apply these concepts immediately to your life while building on what you've previously learned?

Day Ten

Love does not delight in UNRIGHTEOUSNESS.

The Greek phrase *ou chairó adikia* literally translated means: love does not lean towards and give favor to injustice or hurt. We are wonderful at defending others when we feel they've been hurt, scorned, or treated unjustly. Oh, but we have less to say when it comes to ourselves. Suddenly, it's OK, and we'll often just "take it on the chin." Even a step further—it's easy to say, "Well, maybe I did something to deserve that." Rather than face the conflict of standing up for ourselves, we lean into, favor, and relax in the wrong, hurt, or injustice. We love to say, "It's easier that way," or assign our own reasons for other people's actions and wrongdoing.

Today, I challenge you not to lean towards and give grace and favor to injustice enacted against you. I challenge you not to delight in or be OK with wrongdoing. I challenge you to love yourself enough to stand for yourself, speak for yourself, and require the love and respect you deserve in ALL of your relationships. *That's* love.

Reflections

1. How did you apply yesterday's concept to your life, and how did that work out?

Reflections

2. What did today's entry reveal to you about how you love yourself, and how did that make you feel?

_____

_____

_____

_____

_____

_____

_____

_____

_____

_____

_____

_____

_____

_____

_____

_____

Reflections

3. What is one practical way to apply these concepts immediately to your life while building on what you've previously learned?

You've reached Day 10, but this is not the end. You are well on your way, but this is a journey we all <u>must</u> embark on *daily with intention*. Every single day, there are opportunities to detour from the path of profound self-love, but it is up to us to stay the course.

1 Corinthians 13:17, 18a
Love bears all things, believes all things, hopes all things, and endures all things. Love never fails.

To bear – to cover closely, like a lid on a water bottle, ensuring nothing spills out.

To believe – to be persuaded and certain.

To hope – to expect and actively wait for fulfillment.

To endure – to remain, hold/stand ground, and push back [against].

To fail – to submit, bow to condemnation.

You must always contain and hold close your self-love. You must be persuaded and certain of your self-love. You must expect and actively wait for the benefits of your self-love. You must stand fast and push against ANY enemy of your self-love, and you must NEVER submit or bow down to the doubt and fear that would try to rob you of your self-love. It is your divine right to love yourself PROFOUNDLY. *That's love!*

Made in the USA
Columbia, SC
16 September 2022